Earth's Oceans

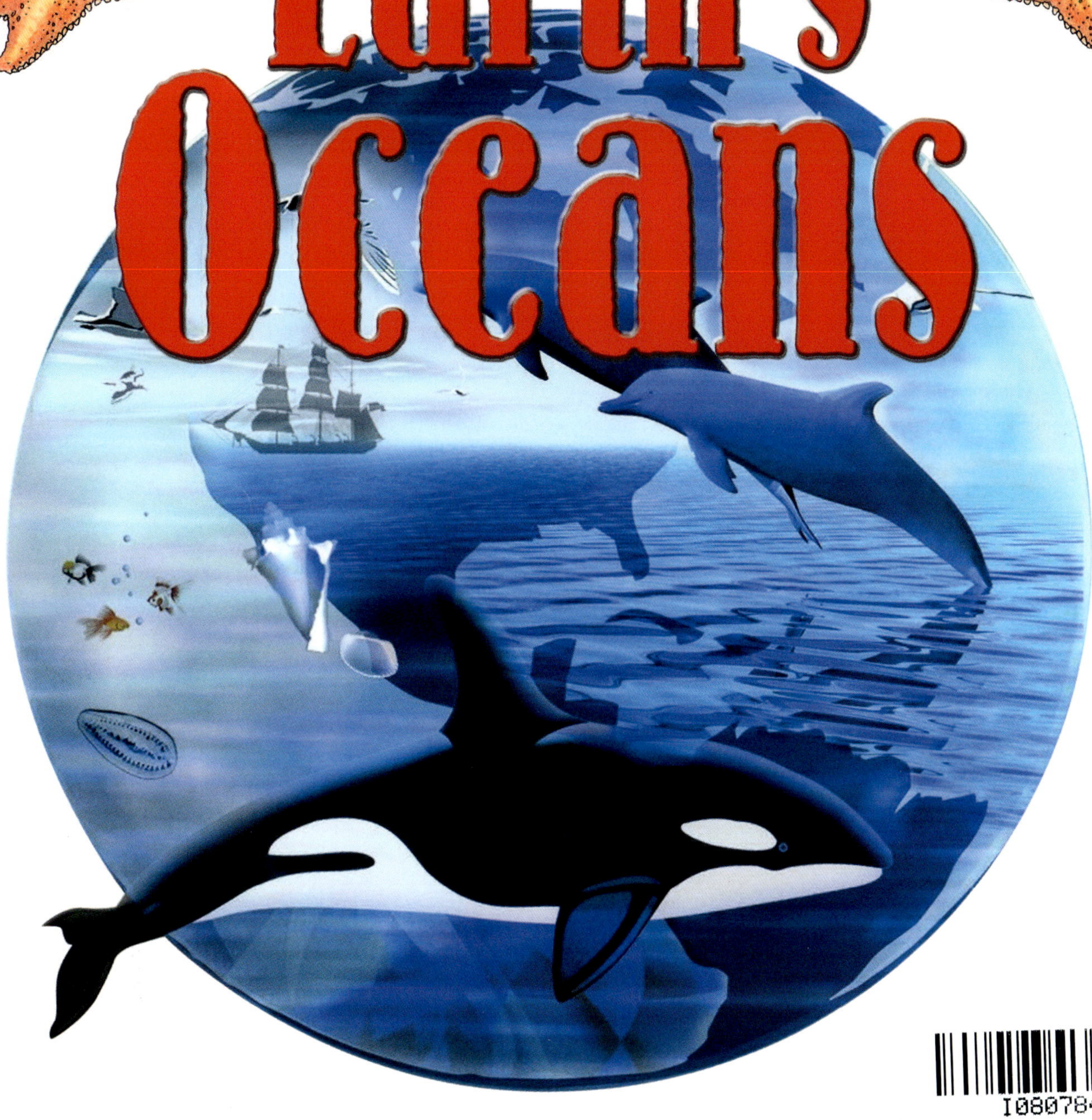

Bobbie Kalman and Kelley MacAulay

Crabtree Publishing Company

www.crabtreebooks.com

Created by Bobbie Kalman

For my cousin Pat Girouard,
with much love and admiration

Editor-in-Chief
Bobbie Kalman

Writing team
Bobbie Kalman
Kelley MacAulay

Editor
Robin Johnson

Copy editor
Michael Hodge

Photo research
Bobbie Kalman
Crystal Sikkens

Design
Katherine Berti
Samantha Crabtree (cover)

Production coordinator
Katherine Berti

Illustrations
Barbara Bedell: pages 1, 4 (jellyfish, white fish, crayfish, and seal), 5 (left sea horse), 12 (bottom fish), 13 (shark), 23, 28 (sea lion), 29, 30 (all except yellow fish and crab)
Tammy Everts: page 5 (feather duster worms)
Katherine Berti: pages 4 (blue and yellow fish), 5 (right sea horse), 6 (walrus), 12 (all except fish) 13 (all except shark), 30 (yellow fish and crab)
Cori Marvin: page 12 (top fish)
Jeannette McNaughton-Julich: page 4 (whale and dolphin)
Trevor Morgan: page 6 (seal)
Vanessa Parson-Robbs: page 26
Bonna Rouse: pages 4 (sea turtle), 5 (starfish and sea fan)
Margaret Amy Salter: pages 5 (bottom left), 6 (octopus), 28 (crab)

Photographs
© iStockphoto.com: page 28
© Richard Herrmann / SeaPics.com: page 14
© Shutterstock.com: cover, pages 1, 3, 4-5, 6, 8, 9, 10, 11, 15, 16, 17, 18, 19, 20, 21, 22, 24, 25, 26, 27, 29, 30 (top), 31
Other images by Digital Stock and Digital Vision

Library and Archives Canada Cataloguing in Publication

Kalman, Bobbie, 1947-
Earth's oceans / Bobbie Kalman & Kelley MacAulay.

(Looking at earth)
Includes index.
ISBN 978-0-7787-3204-4 (bound).--ISBN 978-0-7787-3214-3 (pbk)

1. Ocean--Juvenile literature. 2. Marine biology--Juvenile literature. I. MacAulay, Kelley II. Title. III. Series.

GC21.5.K34 2008 j551.46 C2008-900470-1

Library of Congress Cataloging-in-Publication Data

Kalman, Bobbie.
Earth's oceans / Bobbie Kalman and Kelley MacAulay.
p. cm. -- (Looking at earth)
Includes index.
ISBN-13: 978-0-7787-3214-3 (pbk. : alk. paper)
ISBN-10: 0-7787-3214-2 (pbk. : alk. paper)
ISBN-13: 978-0-7787-3204-4 (reinforced library binding : alk. paper)
ISBN-10: 0-7787-3204-5 (reinforced library binding : alk. paper)
1. Ocean--Juvenile literature. I. MacAulay, Kelley. II. Title.

GC21.5.K35 2008
551.46--dc22
2008002443

Crabtree Publishing Company

Printed in the U.S.A./102012/CJ20120907

www.crabtreebooks.com 1-800-387-7650

Published in Canada
Crabtree Publishing
616 Welland Ave.
St. Catharines, Ontario
L2M 5V6

Published in the United States
Crabtree Publishing
PMB 59051
350 Fifth Avenue, 59th Floor
New York, New York 10118

Published in the United Kingdom
Crabtree Publishing
Maritime House
Basin Road North, Hove
BN41 1WR

Published in Australia
Crabtree Publishing
3 Charles Street
Coburg North
VIC, 3058

Contents

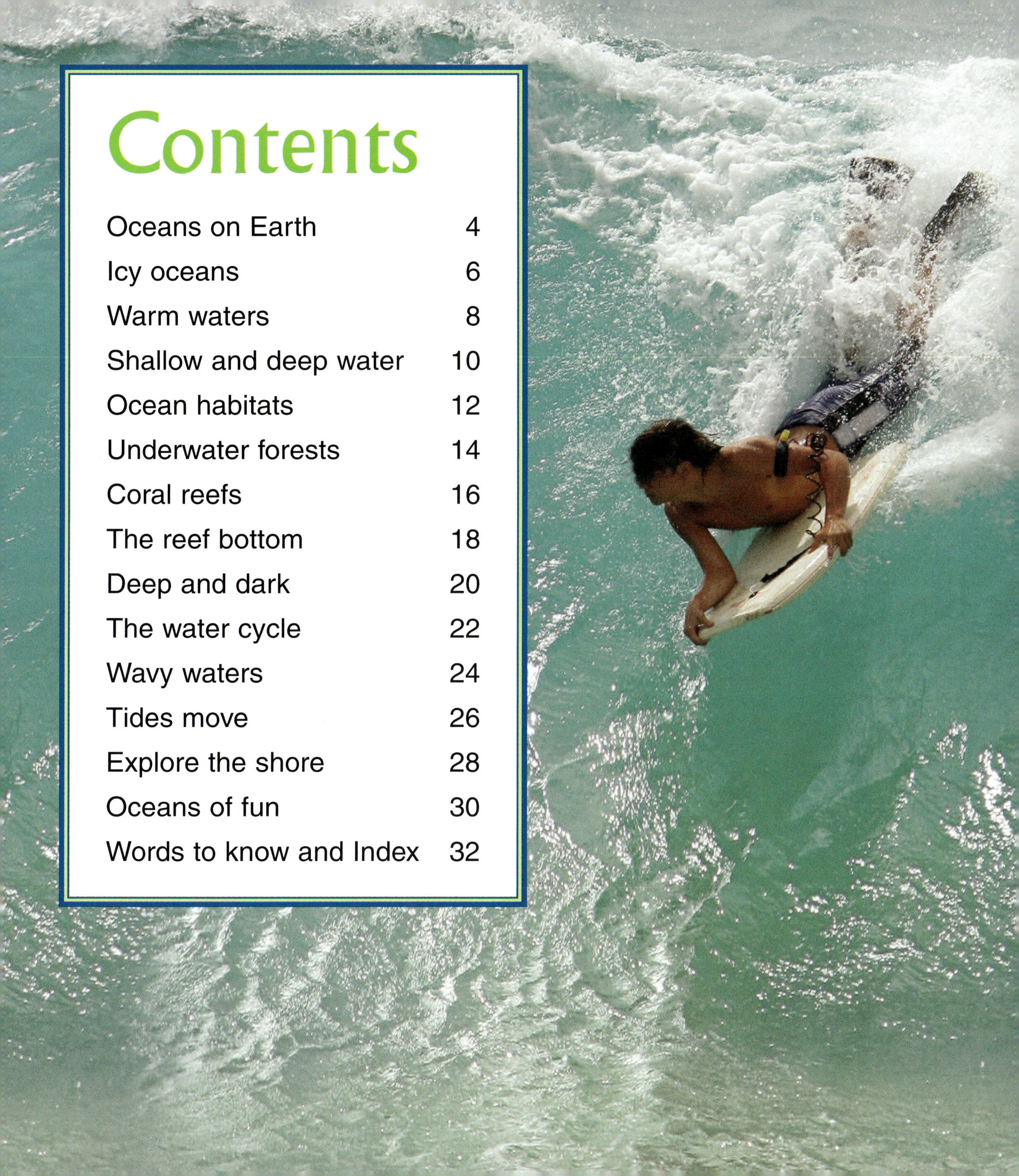

Oceans on Earth

Three-quarters of Earth is covered by water. Most of the water is in **oceans**. Oceans are huge areas of water. The water in oceans is **salt water**. Salt water has a lot of salt in it.

The oceans flow around the seven ***continents****. Continents are very large areas of land. The continents are North America, South America, Europe, Asia, Africa, Australia and Oceania, and Antarctica.*

The five oceans

There are five oceans. The three largest oceans are the Pacific Ocean, the Atlantic Ocean, and the Indian Ocean. The two smaller oceans are the Arctic Ocean and the Southern Ocean.

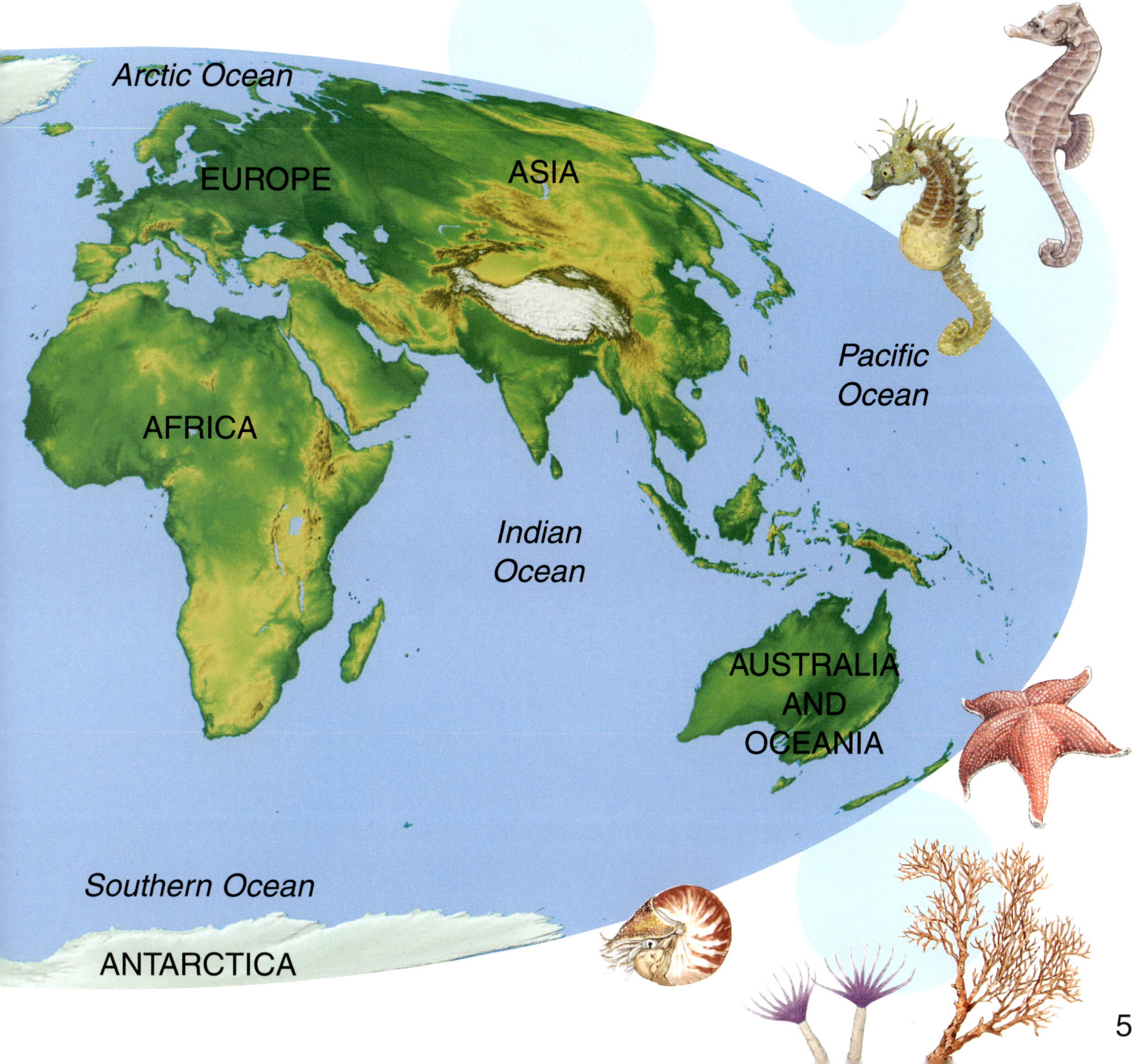

Icy oceans

The weather is always cold near the top and the bottom of Earth. The Arctic Ocean is at the top of Earth. The Southern Ocean is near the bottom of Earth. These oceans are freezing cold.

Walruses, octopuses, seals, and polar bears find food in the Arctic Ocean.

Cold as ice

Cold oceans have a lot of ice. Some of the ice is in huge sheets. Other ice is in big chunks. Chunks of ice are called **icebergs**. Penguins, seals, and other animals rest on icebergs. They look for food in the cold ocean waters.

These penguins and seals are resting on icebergs in the Southern Ocean.

Warm waters

The **equator** is an imaginary line around Earth's center. The weather is always hot near the equator. Big parts of the Pacific Ocean, the Atlantic Ocean, and the Indian Ocean are in this hot area. Ocean waters near the equator are always warm.

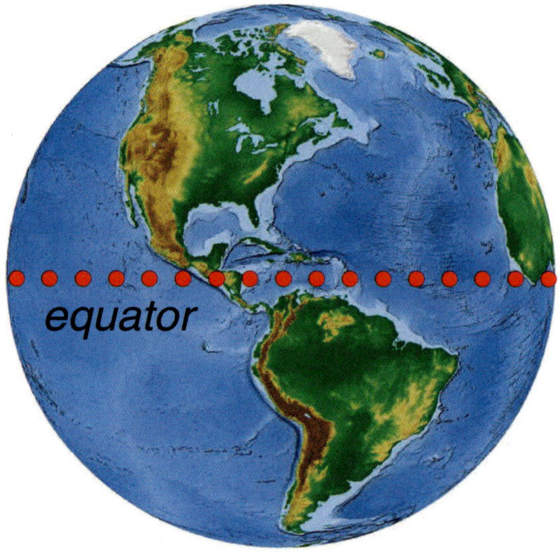

Warm ocean waters are clear and bright blue.

This shore is rocky. It has no sandy beach.

Sandy and rocky

A **shore** is land along the edge of an ocean. Many shores around warm oceans are sandy beaches. Some shores are both sandy and rocky. The shore above is in Australia. The rocks in the water were formed by ocean waves.

Shallow and deep water

The water that is near a shore is shallow. The water that is far from a shore is deep. Ocean waters that are far from shores are very deep.

This girl is playing in shallow water at a sandy beach.

Deep ocean waters look dark.
Shallow ocean waters
look light blue or green.

In shallow ocean waters,
the sun reaches the
bottom of the water.
In deep ocean waters, only the
top part of the water is sunny.
The bottom part of the water is dark.

Ocean habitats

Oceans are **habitats**. Habitats are places in nature where plants grow and animals live. Plants grow in sunny parts of oceans. They need sunlight to make food. Making food from sunlight is called **photosynthesis**. These seaweeds are making food. Seaweeds are plants that grow in ocean habitats.

An ocean food chain

Animals that live in ocean habitats find plenty of food to eat. Some ocean animals eat plants. Most ocean animals eat other animals. When an animal eats another animal that has eaten a plant, there is a **food chain**. This food chain is made up of sea plants, a blue tang, and a shark.

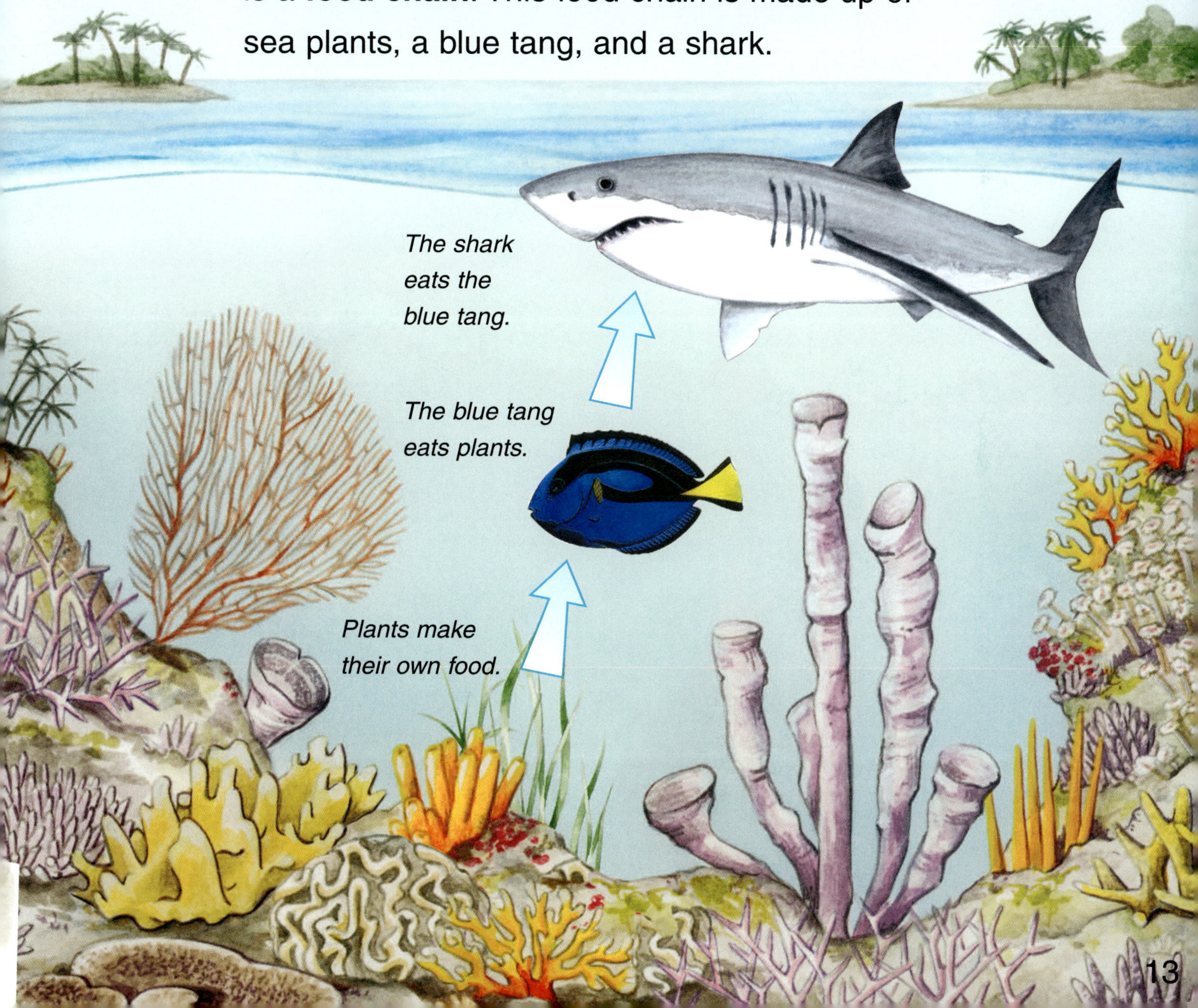

Underwater forests

Kelp forests are ocean habitats. They are made up of tall ocean plants called **kelp**. Kelp forests grow near the shores of cool oceans. They are not found in the very warm parts of the oceans. Whales, octopuses, crabs, and many kinds of fish find food in kelp forests.

This gray whale is swimming through a kelp forest.

Floating over kelp

Sea otters float in the water above kelp forests. They float, even while they are sleeping. Before sea otters go to sleep, they wrap kelp around their bodies. The kelp keeps the otters from floating away in the ocean! Sea otters spend almost all of their time in water.

kelp

These sleeping sea otters have wrapped kelp around their bodies.

Coral reefs

Coral reefs are ocean habitats with many kinds of fish and other animals. Coral reefs are found near the shores of warm oceans. They are made up of **corals**. Corals look like colorful plants, but they are not plants. They are groups of tiny animals called **coral polyps**.

These coral polyps look like flowers.

What is hiding at the bottom of this coral reef? It is a fish called a moray eel!

Around islands

Many coral reefs are found near **islands**. An island is land that has water all around it. This reef is very close to shore. The water is shallow. The reef gets plenty of sun.

The reef bottom

In most coral reefs, even the bottom of the ocean gets sunlight. Many kinds of animals live there. Some animals move, and some cannot move. Tube sponges and many kinds of corals are animals that cannot move. These animals stay in one place their whole lives. They wait for the water to carry food to them.

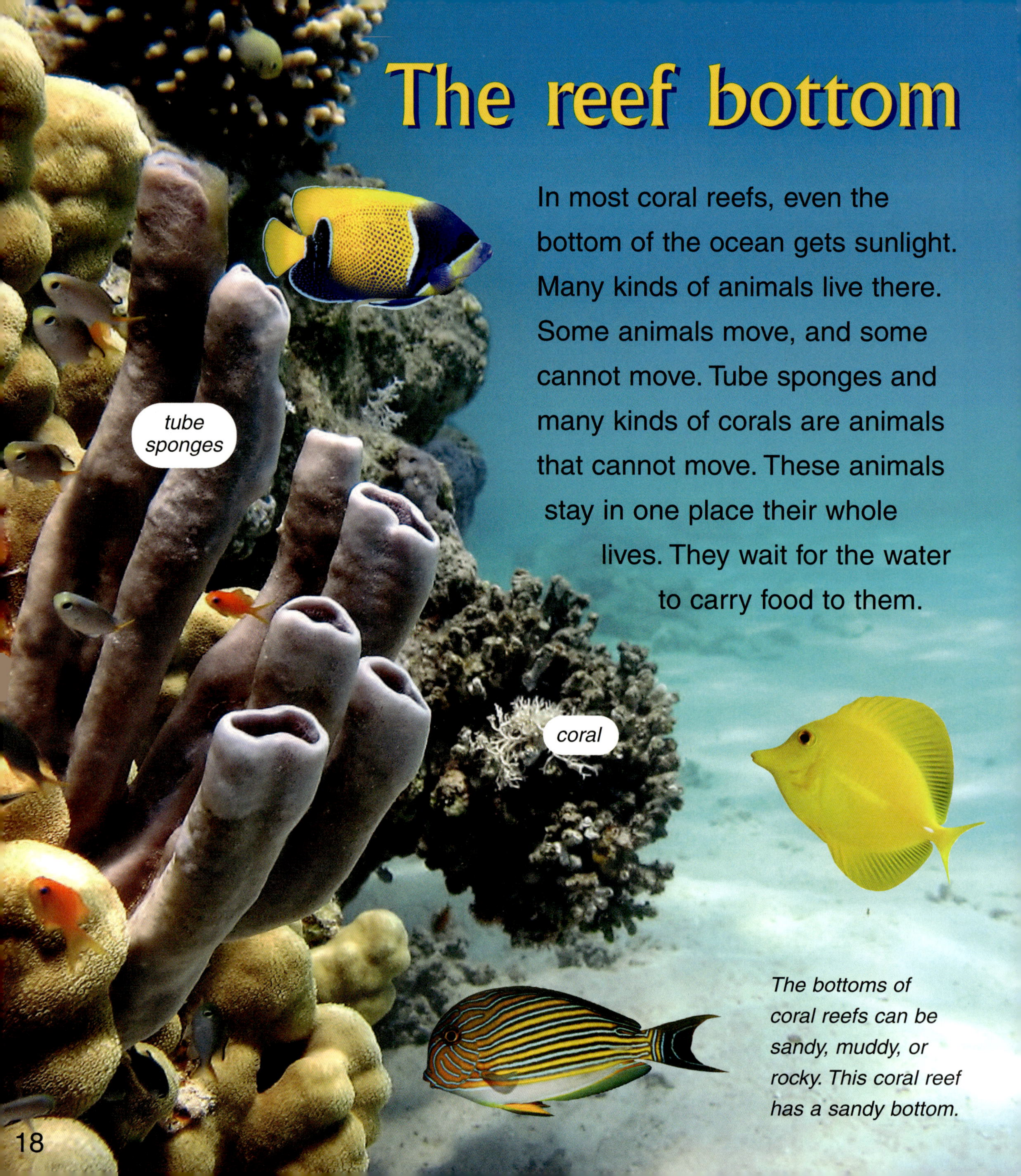

The bottoms of coral reefs can be sandy, muddy, or rocky. This coral reef has a sandy bottom.

On the move

Some ocean animals do not stay in one place. They swim from place to place looking for food. This leopard shark is searching for some fish to eat. The fish below have found a place to hide. They are inside a small cave at the bottom of a reef. Does the shark see them?

Deep and dark

This squid lives in deep, dark ocean waters.

The deep parts of all oceans are dark. Sunlight does not reach these areas. The water is freezing cold. Very few animals can live in these cold, dark waters. Octopuses, sea jellies, and squids are animals that live in the deep parts of oceans.

Lighting up

Many animals that live in the dark parts of oceans can make their own light. The animals make light so other animals will find them. Then they eat the other animals.

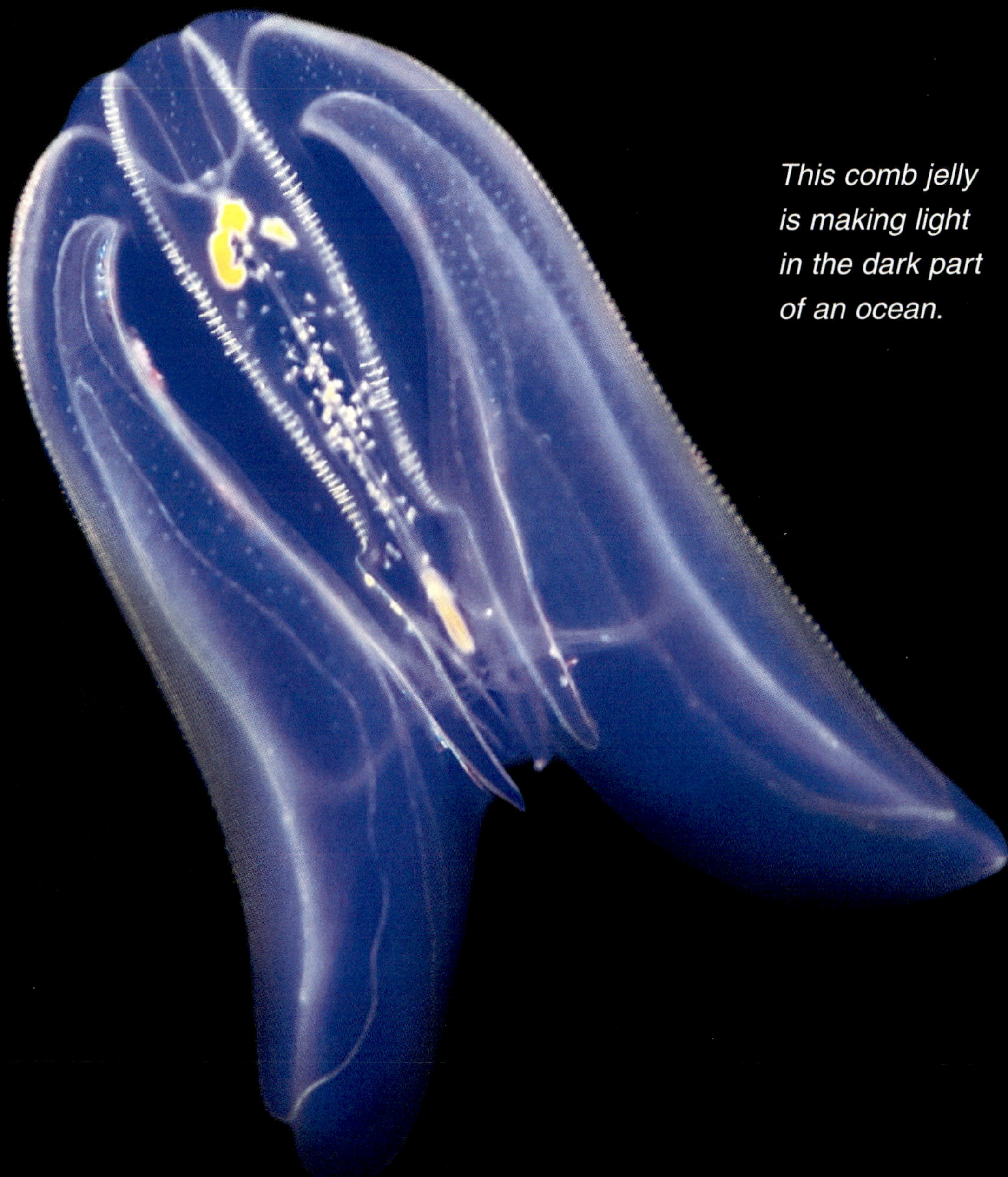

This comb jelly is making light in the dark part of an ocean.

The water cycle

Water is always moving. Water moves as it changes **form**. Form is the way something looks. Water can be **liquid**, **solid**, or **vapor**. Water moves up to the sky as vapor. It falls back down to Earth as rain or snow. Water moving into the air and back to Earth is called the **water cycle**.

Around and around

The sun and wind move water. Water becomes part of the clouds, part of the ground, and part of rivers and lakes. Over time, all water returns to the oceans. Some water flows back to oceans in rivers. Some water falls into oceans as rain or snow.

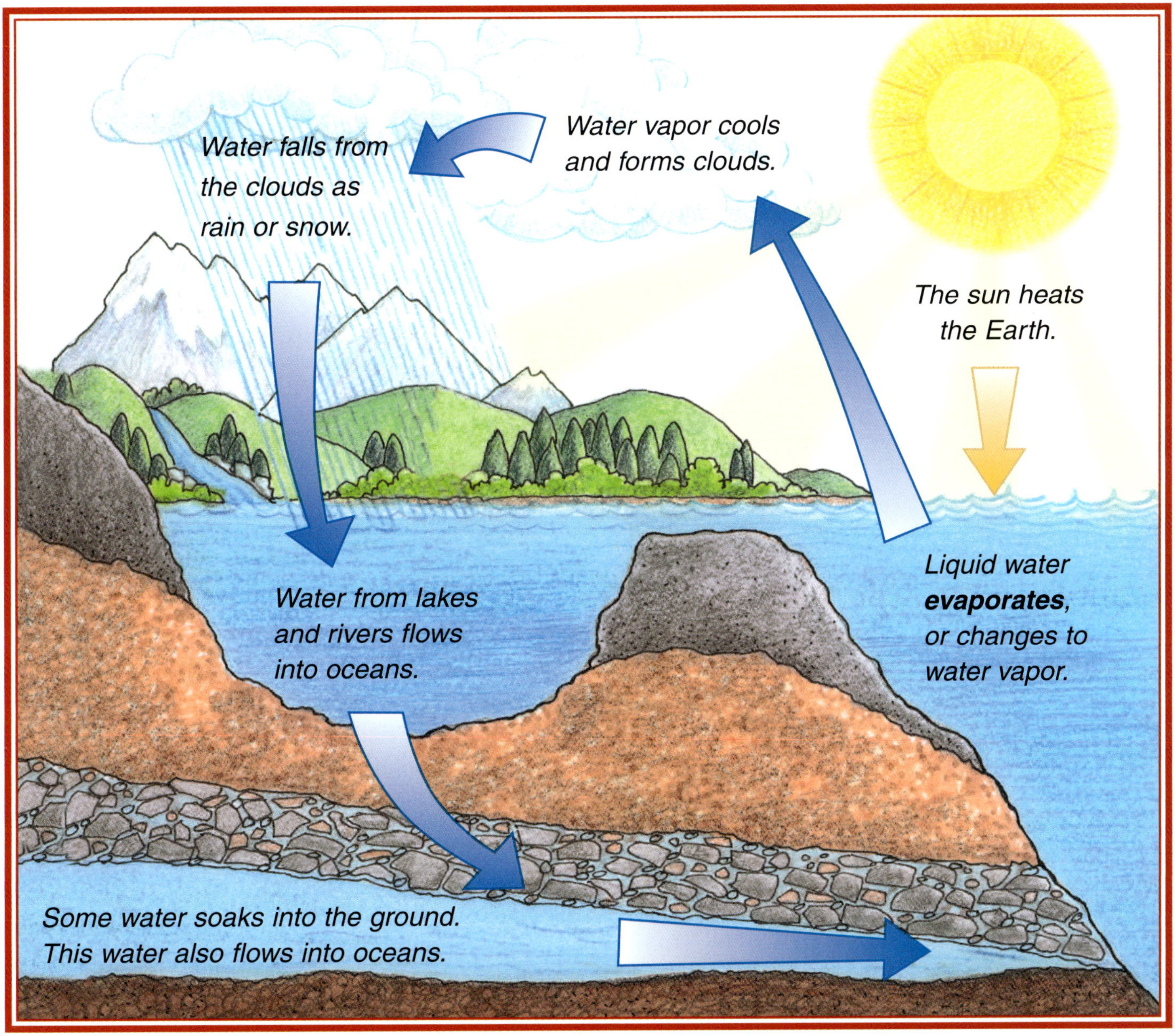

Wavy waters

Ocean water is always moving, too. Wind blows across the top of oceans. The wind pushes the water. The water moves in waves. Some waves are small. Other waves are big. It is fun to play in ocean waves. This boy is riding a small wave.

Dangerous waves

Some waves are like big walls of water. The huge waves in this picture were part of a **hurricane**. A hurricane is a big storm with strong winds. Hurricanes start in oceans. Strong winds cause huge ocean waves to crash onto the shore. The waves destroy buildings and damage the land.

Tides move

Ocean water moves onto the shore twice each day. It also moves off of the shore twice each day. Ocean water moving onto the shore and off the shore is called **tides**.

In or out?

The **tide is in** when ocean water covers the shore. The **tide is out** when ocean water does not cover the shore. Is the tide in or out in the picture below? What clues helped you with your answer?

In this picture, the tide is in. Most of the shore is covered by water.

In this picture, the tide is out. Most of the shore is not covered by water.

Explore the shore

Shores are very big when the tide is out. Some shores are muddy, and others are rocky. There are animals on the shores. Seals and sea lions rest on shores. Crabs crawl along shores. Birds run on shores, looking for crabs to eat.

sea lion

crab

This seagull has found a crab to eat on a shore. The shore is covered with small stones.

Waiting for the tide

When the tide is out, some water stays in small pools on the shore. The pools are called **tide pools**. Some ocean animals get trapped in tide pools. The animals cannot move from the pools until the tide comes in. Animals that are trapped in tide pools are often eaten by other animals.

These sea anemones, sea urchins, and sea stars are in a tide pool.

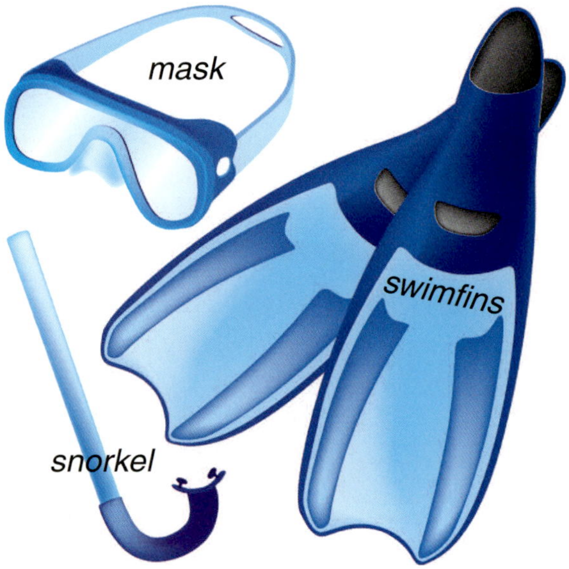

Oceans of fun

This boy is **snorkeling** in the ocean. Snorkeling is swimming with a snorkel, mask, and swimfins. It is a great way to learn about the creatures that live in the ocean. How much do you know about ocean animals? Take this quiz and find out!

Which animal is...

1. a dolphin?
2. a crab?
3. a clownfish?
4. a leafy sea dragon?
5. a parrotfish?
6. a butterflyfish?
7. a sea turtle?
8. Which three animals are not fish?

Answers: 1—G; 2—F; 3—B; 4—C; 5—E; 6—D; 7—A; 8—A, F, and G

Words to know

Note: Some boldfaced words are defined where they appear in the book.

continent One of the seven large areas of land on Earth

coral The hard outer covering of an animal that forms coral reefs

equator An imaginary line around the middle of Earth

hurricane A huge storm with strong winds and heavy rains

kelp A brown seaweed that can grow very large and form forests in oceans

liquid Something that flows freely

photosynthesis The use of sunlight by plants to turn air and water into food

solid Something with a firm shape

tide pool Rocky areas at the edges of oceans that trap sea creatures when the tide is out

vapor A substance that has changed from a liquid and become part of air

Index